Motivating Thoughts Of Chanakya

Edited by
SHIKHA SHARMA

PRABHAT
PRAKASHAN

Published by
PRABHAT PRAKASHAN PVT. LTD.
4/19 Asaf Ali Road,
New Delhi-110002 (INDIA)
e-mail: prabhatbooks@gmail.com

ISBN 978-93-5521-775-2
MOTIVATING THOUGHTS OF CHANAKYA
Edited by Shikha Sharma

Edition
First, 2023

Price
₹ 250 (Rupees Two Hundred Fifty Only)

Printed at
Japan Art, Delhi

Editor's Note

Chanakya, also known as Vishnugupta and Kautilya, is known as a grand thinker and scholar of ancient times whose exploits led to the rise of Chandragupta Maurya as the first-ever emperor of India. He groomed the young Chandragupta Maurya, to make him a resplendent personality, efficient ruler and able warrior. It was the framework of the policies set by Chanakya that India flourished to become a great nation.

Chanakya has written his opus magnum, Arthashastra, a fine treatise on politics. The policies set by him are called Chanakya Neeti, which are referred to even today to resolve and understand the prevailing issues. This might be an ancient work, yet it has retained its contemporary value by the wisdom and virtue it contains, hence the need to know what he has written.

In his book, Chanakya has dealt with a wide variety of subjects under the sun, and it is worthwhile to know the expanse of his learnings, knowledge, thinking and wisdom; this is like an ocean from which we can draw food for thought and advice for action in all circumstances that we may confront in our daily life.

In this book, we have made a solemn endeavour to compile his views on different topics. It is a delight to read them and follow them as well. Thus, making him the greatest motivational guru we have ever seen.

❑

Contents

❑

A Brief Biography of Chanakya

No conclusive detail is available anywhere in history about the birthplace and date of birth of the world-famous diplomat and statesman, Chanakya. It is estimated that he was born in 350 BC. Some scholars even say that he was born in 400 BC.

However, there is no unanimity among historians about his birthplace and date of birth, but we do find unanimity among scholars regarding his outstanding role in consolidating the foundation of the Maurya dynasty and in making Chandragupta an Emperor. Therefore, he was definitely born before Chandragupta.

It is said that the name of Chanakya's father was Chanak. Therefore, he was known as 'Chanakya.' His actual name was Vishnugupta. Since he was born in the Kutila lineage, he was known as 'Kautilya'.

There are several stories about the early life of Chanakya. According to one such story, Chanakya was dark-complexioned and not good-looking. Once when his mother started weeping while looking at his face,

Chanakya asked her the reason for her distress. She said, "Son, you will grow up to be a king and forget me. I am unable to hold my tears as I think about it." Chanakya was startled by her mother's reply. He asked her again, "How do you know that I shall grow up to be a king?" "Your pair of front teeth indicate it," his mother replied.

Chanakya instantly went out and broke his pair of front teeth with a stone. He came back to his mother and said, "Look! I have broken my front teeth. How shall I become a king now? Therefore, you need not worry. I shall neither become a king nor forsake you." It appears from the story that Chanakya was a very tender-hearted and emotional person. Also, he was deeply attached to his mother. On the other hand, there is another story.

According to it, Chanakya had a tough temperament. He could not bear insults. He was a man of self-respect. He was determined and persistent.

Once when Chanakya was going somewhere, on the way, he stepped on a thorn in the Kusha grass. The thorn pierced through and wounded his foot. It became difficult for him to walk ahead. A determined Chanakya then and there pulled the Kusha grass off its roots. He continued to pull the grass off its roots. After this, he poured acid over its roots so that they could not germinate again.

It is difficult to verify the truth in this story, but it indicates the magnitude of his anger. At the same time, it also indicates that he was capable of doing whatever he decided to do.

Chanakya was educated at Takshashila. Takshashila was a world-famous university in those days. Students from far and near came there to study. Generally, the princes used to study there. Each of the teachers used to have more than a hundred students under him or her.

The students were taught the four Vedas, archery, elephant and horse riding, eighteen arts and skills, jurisprudence, medicine, politics, social welfare, etc.

Chanakya had also received an education in these subjects. As a result, Chanakya, who was already an intelligent fellow, shone like a polished gem.

After completing his education at Takshashila, Chanakya became a professor of Political Science at the same university. His stature as an excellent scholar spread throughout the country.

Pataliputra was no exception to it. Pataliputra, like Takshashila, was a renowned centre of education.

It was the capital of Magadha. It was ruled by Dhana Nanda. He was a greedy and morally corrupted King. His subjects were not happy with him because he taxed even the objects of wood, stone and leather. However, he had one remarkable quality, that is, he used to honour the well-learned people.

Dhana Nanda had established a committee chaired by a very knowledgeable person to honour scholars and celebrated men. The other members of the committee were also very educated people. It is said that the chairman of the committee had the authority to award ten lakh gold coins to a deserving scholar. Even the junior members of the committee had the authority to award one lakh gold coins.

It is said that Chanakya was invited by the Chairperson of the committee of Pataliputra. When the council requested King Dhana Nanda to appoint Chanakya as chairman, King expressed his desire to meet Chanakya.

When King Dhana Nanda met Chanakya, he was not impressed by his personality because Chanakya was of dark complexion and he was not so good-looking. As a result, the King developed a negative impression of Chanakya. Apart from his unimpressive looks, Chanakya behaved arrogantly towards the King who favoured the sycophants.

Therefore, the King did not honour Chanakya. He refused to appoint him as the Chairperson. He humiliated Chanakya and asked him to get out.

According to another version of the story, Chanakya had come to motivate King Dhana Nanda, in the interest of the nation, in order to unite the smaller states into one, because Dhana Nanda was the strongest ruler of the largest empire. But Dhana Nanda did not favour his proposal. He humiliated Chanakya by asking him to leave the court.

Whatever may be the truth, the fact remains that King Dhana Nanda had insulted Chanakya, as a result of which he became very angry. As per his temperamental nature, Chanakya untied his locked hair and vowed not to tie them again until Dhana Nanda was removed from the throne.

When King Dhana Nanda heard of Chanakya's vow, his blood boiled in rage. He ordered his men to arrest Chanakya, but Chanakya had already left before he could be arrested. Chanakya put on the robes of a mendicant and continued to live in Pataliputra secretly.

One day, Chanakya saw Chandragupta, who as a boy then, playing the game of king and subjects with his friends.

Chanakya was impressed by Chandragupta. He discovered that Chandragupta has the potential of a great king in him. Chanakya enquired about Chandragupta and bought him after paying his guardians 1,000 karshapanas. He took him to Takshashila.

At Takshashila, Chanakya taught Chandragupta everything—from the Vedas to warfare and politics. After tutoring him for eight years, Chanakya transformed him into a brave warrior.

At the same time, Alexander the Great was approaching India after defeating all the kings who were coming his way. Alexander had been invited to India by King Ambhi of Gandhar. Ambhi wanted to settle scores with his old enemy Porus, while Alexander wanted to return to his native kingdom with the booty he would get after plundering India and enslaving the innocent people here. But King Ambhi did not care about that.

When Chanakya came to know of Ambhi's plans, he met Ambhi and gave him a piece of sound advice. He explained to him the consequences that could befall due to his move, but Ambhi did not pay heed to the words of Chanakya. He remained firm in his stand to assist Alexander.

After a few days, when Alexander entered Gandhar, Ambhi arranged for a huge assembly in honour of Alexander. Along with the important citizens, students and professors of Takshashila University were also invited to the assembly.

Chanakya and his disciple Chandragupta were also present in the assembly. There, Alexander was highly praised in the speeches. He was compared to the gods.

Alexander subtly threatened the Indians in his speech that they should accept his supremacy for their own welfare.

Alexander's threat was countered by Chanakya through his well-organised and balanced speech. Chanakya wanted to protect his countrymen from the invasion of foreigners.

In the assembly, Chandragupta also wanted to raise his voice in favour of Chanakya, but Chanakya refrained Chandragupta from doing anything. Although Alexander was impressed by the ideas and policies of Chanakya yet he did not want to be distracted from his goal of global conquest.

After the end of the assembly, Chanakya organised a group of 500 students of Takshashila University with the help of Chandragupta and met King Porus or Puru. King Porus was the enemy of Ambhi. As the saying goes 'An enemy of an enemy is a friend.' Therefore, Chanakya easily got the support of King Porus in the interest of the nation.

Soon, Alexander attacked Porus (Puru). King Porus had the support of Chanakya and Chandragupta. Therefore, he was highly spirited. The war proved difficult for Alexander's army. Suddenly, King Porus' elephant turned wild and ran helter-skelter, causing confusion among Porus' soldiers. Alexander made the best use of this opportunity and imprisoned Porus.

Later on, Alexander entered into a treaty with King Porus.

Chanakya thought now it was wise to distance himself from Porus. Later, Chanakya met the other kings and encouraged them to wage a war against Alexander.

Meanwhile, an internal revolt occurred within Alexander's army. The warriors had, for long, been separated from their families. They were tired of the war. Therefore, they wanted to go back to their respective homes. In India itself, several kings, under the leadership of Chanakya and Chandragupta, had begun raising their heads against Alexander. Therefore, Alexander decided to go back to Greece. A few days later, Alexander died of a disease.

The only task before Chanakya was to avenge his humiliation by Dhana Nanda. Meanwhile, Chandragupta had organised an army of nationalist Kshatriyas. Therefore, Chanakya instigated Chandragupta to attack Magadha.

Chanakya's diplomatic moves ensured Chandragupta's victory over Magadha. King Dhana Nanda was killed in the war.

Chanakya declared Chandragupta as the Emperor of Magadha, who was warmly welcomed. Chandragupta wanted to appoint his Guru Chanakya as his Mahamatya (Prime Minister). But Chanakya didn't accept this post. He wanted this post to be held by Rakshasa, the earlier Mahamatya of Magadha. But Rakshasa went into hiding and was waiting for an occasion to avenge the death of Dhana Nanda.

Chanakya was aware of Rakshasa's intention. He pressed the services of his secret agents into full use. After concerted diplomatic efforts, he was successful in arresting Rakshasa. But Chanakya did not punish Rakshasa, instead, he advised Chandragupta to pardon him and appoint him to the post of Mahamatya.

Chandragupta could not disobey his guru. He appointed Rakshasa as his Mahamatya.

Later on, Chanakya constructed a hut for himself on the bank of River Ganga and stayed there. From his humble abode, Chanakya used to make state policies and advise Chandragupta from time to time.

After establishing the empire, Guru Chanakya composed Arthashastra, a great work on statecraft. He was a master of the three Vedas, the Shastras, the science of mantras, diplomacy and politics. Moreover, he was a great scholar of various subjects and a philosopher as well.

He used his in-depth knowledge of statecraft to unite the scattered Indians into a great nation. Despite establishing the vast and great Maurya empire, he was unattached to power and pelf. Instead of living in the comfortable palace of Pataliputra, he used to live in a humble cottage on the bank of River Ganga and cook his own food.

In due course, the Maurya empire established by Chanakya became a great empire, extending from Gandhar in the west to Bengal in the east and from Kashmir in the north to Mysore in the south. Chandragupta ruled for about 24 years under Chanakya's guidance. The Arthashastra composed by Chanakya is reckoned among the great works of the world. There are about 5,000 verses in this book related to statecraft. There are 15 chapters and several sub-chapters in it.

The sutras described in Chanakya Neeti are even today used as the guiding principles.

Like his birth details, there is also no conclusive evidence about his death.

❑

Quotes of Chanakya

Action

- When the right action is not taken at the right time, then it is time itself that causes the action to fail.
- One can't escape the consequence of an action, no matter what one may do.
- Those born blind cannot see; similarly blind are those in the grip of lust. Proud men have no perception of evil, and those bent on acquiring riches see no sin in their actions.
- A person alone has to bear the consequences of all his good and bad deeds. He has no partner in this. Happiness and sorrow are only his; they will affect him and no other. He has to travel life's journey towards heaven alone.

- For his salvation, a man must keep trying himself.
- A criminal may be breathing but he is like a dead person. On the other hand, a person performing auspicious and good deeds is remembered even after his death. His reputation and fame keep him alive well after he is dead.
- A man's consciousness is stirred after performing evil or derogatory actions and the feeling of regret sets in. But if he realizes what is good and what is bad before indulging in them, he will not be trapped in bad deeds at all.
- Fate is not in a person's hands, but his actions certainly are.
- If there is a slip in religious performance, it does not yield any reward. If a life-saving medicine is not used as directed, it can prove life-threatening. Excessive wastage of food and wealth leads to poverty.
- An improper act committed by an influential person seems proper to people. Against this, even a proper act performed by an inadequate person draws suspicion from the people.
- Before starting any job, weigh all the possible pros and cons and then decide your course of action.
- A man himself invites sorrow in his life through his actions.

Addiction

- A person addicted to liquor is like a blind man. Intoxicated by liquor, people lose their mental balance and ability to think rationally.
- Anyone addicted to gambling can never complete his or her project.

Aim

- A person, who leads an aimless life, can neither find peace at home nor in the forest. His life is like a dead weight on the earth benefiting no one.
- A person who has decided on his life's aim could never go astray.

Anger

- A moment of patience in a moment of anger can help us avoid a thousand moments of sorrow.
- Anger ruins a person completely. It is like the image of the god of Death, which is ever ready to grasp the person in its hideous jaws. Under its influence, a person loses his mental equilibrium and it leads to performing despicable acts.
- A harsh word spoken in anger can be so toxic that it can destroy your thousand lovely moments in minutes.

Arrogance

- A man should not grow arrogant over his capability of donation, devotion, bravery, worship, courage, knowledge of science, politeness and strategic prowess. Anyone who becomes arrogant, sins in a hurry and is ruined.
- An arrogant person is one who gets everything without hard work. On the other hand, a hard-working person also respects the hard work of others.

Attachment

- He who is overly attached to his family members, experiences fear and sorrow, for the root of all grief is attachment. Thus, one should discard attachments to be happy.
- When a man develops an attachment to someone, his life is guided by that person. When that person is unhappy, he is also unhappy. Similarly, he feels happy and scared according to the person he is attached to.
- Drop the idea that attachment and love are one thing. They are enemies. It is the attachment that destroys all love.

❑

B

Bathing

- After the oil massage, a visit to the crematorium, conjugation and shaving, a man's body becomes impure. The act of bathing purifies him again, so after the above-cited acts, it is essential to take a bath. It is also healthy.
- One must not bathe immediately after mating as it is not healthy.

Begging

- If a person goes to anyone's house as a beggar, his respect, honour and pride are ruined. Therefore, a man should work hard, so that the need to beg does not arise.
- A blade of straw and cotton are the lightest things in this world. But a beggar is figuratively still lighter than these two.

Behaviour

- A man's behaviour is enough to make people bow before him. Even enemies can be won over.
- A drunkard loses control over his speech. So, it is difficult to predict how he will behave.
- Public dealings cover polite behaviour with servants, affectionate behaviour with relations and tough behaviour with evil persons. In addition, it covers affectionate and gentle behaviour towards gentlemen and scholars, a courageous stand against enemies, enduring and respectful behaviour towards teachers and witty behaviour towards women. Anyone with such behaviour will lead a happy life in society.
- Spending more than your earnings, fighting with others without any reason and mating with all types of women—these three acts propel man and his family towards ruin.
- Without too much effort, only by good conduct and disposition a man can satisfy a scholar, a gentleman and a father. Similarly, by sweet talk, he can please and satisfy friends, relatives and scholars. For a person with good behaviour and sweet talk, nothing is impossible.
- Apart from the body structure, there is not much difference between man and animal; it is only his behaviour that makes him superior to animals.

Being Yourself

- Be yourself because no one else can always do it better than you can.
- Don't worry about being different. Just focus on being better.
- If you're not willing to be different, you'll just blend into the crowd.
- It is easy to complicate simple things but it is difficult to simplify complex things. A person who knows how to simplify things is a special person.

Betrayal

- Never rely on someone who is a known betrayer.
- Manners betray one's family and the language of one's country. Hospitality betrays one's love and the physique betrays one's food intake.
- Sharp-clawed beasts, long-horned animals, rapidly-flowing rivers, armed persons, women and relations of royalty are not trustworthy, that is, they can deceive at any time.

Blessed

- Blessed is the mouth that utters sweet speech and by its kind and affectionate sentence destroys the distress of the poor.

- Blessed are those eyes that guide the way of the blind and protect them from their straying on the thorn-ridden paths.
- Blessed are the hands that lend support to helpless persons and help in solving their troubles.
- Like the trees growing their fruits for others' benefit, blessed are those men who devote their lives to others' causes.
- A meeting with a gentleman or a saint can get you their sacred blessings, whereas to get blessings from the holy shrines, we need to undertake long trips.

Body

- Wealth, a friend, a wife and a kingdom may be regained, but this body when lost may never be acquired again.
- The brain controls the body, without it, the body is useless.
- The eyes are the most important part of the body. It is through it that a man is able to see God's beautiful creation.

Books

- Books are as useful to a stupid person as a mirror is useful to a blind person.

Brahmin

- If the Brahmin keeps travelling, he is never short of followers. Also, his status rises in society day by day. Travelling by saints and ascetics enables them to spread their knowledge and wisdom amongst the masses.
- A Brahmin's strength is inherent in his knowledge of the scriptures, through which he can defeat even the greatest scholar.
- At the time of the pralaya (universal destruction), the oceans are to exceed their limits and seek to change, but a saintly man never changes.
- A person who creates obstacles in others' good deeds, who misguides to cheat others and whose atrocities afflict people, such a cruel person, in spite of being a Brahmin, is called a beast.
- A brahmin (scholar) should consume food only once a day and be satisfied with it. Most of his day should be spent conducting Yajna and study of the Vedas.
- A brahmin (scholar) should be able to control delinquencies and mate at the proper time, only for the purpose of producing offspring.

❑

Change

- A person should change according to the prevailing circumstances.

Charity

- A person taking care of others' welfare is pure in the true sense of the term. His soul does not get corrupted even in bad company.
- If the charity is made to a person who is tolerant, learned, honest and gentle, it is received back a hundred times over. However, it should never be given to a person who is lazy, evil, jealous, immoral or sinful, otherwise, such a charity will go useless.
- A man should save and he should also donate. These deeds help him earn respect in society, while he becomes eligible to enjoy unrestricted pleasures in the other world.

- Charity never goes waste. In fact, the donated amount is received back tenfold. So, a man should donate to the needy and scholars in difficulty as much as he can. This will open doors for him to get more wealth.

Children

- For the first five years, a child must be brought up with love and affection. For the next ten years, he must be brought up with strict discipline, because this is the period for the cultivation of his personality and works like the foundation on which rests the rest of his life. From the age of sixteen, he should be treated like a friend; guided like a friend; and his problems should be settled like those of a friend.
- A wise person grooms his child carefully because only an educated person with high morale is given true respect in society.
- Good and bad qualities and conduct of the parents influence their children.
- The parents are able to eliminate their wards' ignorance through their knowledge, so they must build the character of their children. They must develop their talents through proper education and devotion. This will make their children's in-built talents worthy of worship and respect.

- A potter needs to pat, caress and even beat the mud rotating on his wheel to shape it into beautiful pottery. Parents must also bring up and shape their children like a potter shapes his pottery.

Confidence

- A small chain is enough to control a large elephant. A small lamp is enough to erase the darkness. A thunderbolt is enough to crash a large mountain. Your body, shape, size or beauty are not important. Only your strength and confidence are important.

Contentment

- Contentment alone gives complete happiness whereas greed, like sickness, deprives a person of actual happiness.
- One should give up the desire for all kinds of pleasures. Everything is in God's hands—He decides who gets what and who gives what. So, everyone should learn to be satisfied with what he has.
- A man is never contented with wealth, life, woman and delicacies. The more he gets them, the more he feels them insufficient.

Country

- Do not inhabit a country where you are not respected, cannot earn your livelihood, have any friends or cannot acquire knowledge.

- The countries at the border with which we have frequent skirmishes eventually turn into our enemies.

Crisis

- In times of crisis, a man can cross any limits.
- In a time of need, knowledge of books and others' wealth does not help. In a crisis, only the wealth saved by an individual helps.

Criticism

- One who listens to his criticism peacefully gets victory over the world.
- The crow among birds, the dog among animals and a sinner among saints are the evilest and irreligious, the critic is a greater sinner and wretched. A critic gains nothing by criticizing, yet he enjoys it. His sins keep adding up by criticizing and a day comes when his sins destroy none but him.
- Criticizing others is the most depraving and dreadful deed. If a man can give it up, he can control the entire world. By giving up criticism, all the pleasures favour a man.
- Criticizers and backbiters need not be concerned with criminals; they themselves act like criminals by criticizing others.

❑

Death

- A crow, pigeon, sparrow and parrot—despite their being different species and characteristics, sleep on the same tree at night. But at the crack of dawn, they all fly away to their respective destinations. Much like this, the human soul settles in the family-like tree, only to fly away from here at the appointed time. So, one should not grieve or feel sorrow on its departure.
- Death is the law of nature and the entire universe is guided by it. Even the Creator of this world, Lord Brahma cannot change it.

Deeds

- A man is great by deeds not by birth.
- A man is rewarded or punished according to his deeds. Nobody can change this law of nature.

- Everyone reaps the fruits of his deeds, good or bad.
- Man can only control his actions, but only the Lord has the power to reward him for his deeds.
- Sorrow, grief, anxiety and crises, which a man faces in his life, are the consequences of his sinful deeds
- A man's action and its result are linked. So, perform only good deeds to expect favourable rewards.
- As a calf follows its mother among a thousand cows, so the (good or bad) deeds of a man follow him.
- The fulfilment of desires depends on one's fate and actions. His fate decides the rewards based on his actions. If a man wishes for worldly pleasures in return for his bad deeds, his wish will never be fulfilled. So, a person should perform good deeds for favourable rewards.

Dependence

- Being ignorant is painful as it leads to his mockery, but being dependent on someone is most painful. Such a person can be compared to an animal. He has to act on someone else's command.
- A permanent relationship is dependent on a particular purpose or wealth.

Dharma

- The root of Dharma is finance.

Disgrace

- It is better to die than to preserve this life by incurring disgrace. The loss of life causes a moment's grief but disgrace brings grief every day of one's life.
- Being disgraced is more painful and hurting than death.
- A disgraced person is humiliated on every occasion; society views him with hatred; near and dear ones pass derogatory remarks at him. Even his wife and son tend to avoid him. A respectful death gives better relief than living such a life.

❑

E

Education

- Getting an education is like penance. To get it, one should sacrifice the crush of the house and the illusion of magic.
- Appearance, beauty, wealth, property, power, status and youth become graceful only when they are supported by education and wisdom.
- Education is the best friend. An educated person is respected everywhere. Education beats beauty and youth.
- A person should gracefully accept knowledge from wherever he gets it.
- Education is like a hidden treasure, which no one can steal; on the contrary, the more you use it, the more it flourishes.
- Any learning through which you cannot earn money is useless.

- The life of an uneducated man is as useless as the tail of a dog which neither covers its rear end nor protects it from the bites of insects.
- A man must get educated; this will open the doors of progress for him.

Effort

- A person should have complete faith in God, yet he should not shy away from his efforts. God fulfils the wishes only of those who make effort.
- The fate of a man cannot be changed, he has to face whatever is fated, yet by his efforts and actions, the fated adverse circumstances can be turned into favourable circumstances. So, he should not shy away from making efforts.

Enemies

- Till the enemy's weakness is known, he should be kept on friendly terms.
- The enemy's enemy is a friend.
- The quality of the enemy must also be acquired.
- It is necessary for an intelligent person to ensure that his enemies are always trapped in difficulties, so that they may never be able to create any hurdles for him.
- A strong person cannot be overcome by force, yet you can control him by conduct favourable to him. An

evil enemy should be defeated by adopting conduct unfavourable to him; whereas an equal enemy can be overcome by a combination of both humility and force.

- Even a favour done by an enemy can be harmful.
- Fighting against a more powerful enemy is like foot soldiers taking on the elephant brigade. It would be just a suicidal endeavour.
- Keep your enemy deceived by your artificial behaviour till you find his weakness.
- Enemies strike at weak points.

❑

Failure

- Once you start working on something, don't be afraid of failure and abandon it. People who work sincerely are the happiest.

Faith

- Money comes and goes, and so is the youth. Life goes and goes the soul, nothing lasts forever. The only thing that stays firm is your faith.
- One must protect one's faith even at the cost of one's life.

Fate

- Fate follows the man.
- The achievements of knowledgeable or wise persons can also get sullied by the interference of fate or men.
- A person's wisdom is dictated by his fate at birth. His life, actions, situations—everything is decided by

fate. He gets relations and friends as destined by his fate. Man gets only what he is destined to get.

- It is impossible for anyone to overrule his fate. It is the miracle of fate which can turn a king into a pauper and a pauper into a king. Whatever God has in store for man, has to be borne by him and undergo the consequences accordingly. Fate cannot be altered in any manner.
- Even as the unborn baby is in the womb of his mother, these five are fixed as his life destiny: his life span, his activities, his acquisition of wealth and knowledge, and his time of death.
- It is impossible to change what God wills. In his lifetime, a man acts and reaps accordingly. If a bush does not bloom in the spring, it is no fault of the spring; if an owl cannot see during the daytime, it is useless to blame the sun; if the raindrops do not fall in the cuckoo's mouth, it is no fault of the clouds. Similarly, the difficulties and hardships that a man bears during his life, are no fault of his. These are all pre-destined.
- People, who only rely on fate, waste their valuable life. But the persons, who avert crisis through their efforts and continue to confront adverse circumstances, lead a happy life.

Father

- Only a person, who brings up his child properly, and looks after his sorrow and happiness, is fit to be a father, in real terms.
- A father should marry his daughter to a respectable and suitable family. He should also provide the best possible education to his son.
- By pampering and accepting all the right or wrong demands of their children, a father may cultivate several bad habits in his children. These bad habits hinder their progress and development in the future. It is, therefore, essential to discipline them too.

Faults

- He who points out others' flaws in the people's court or parliament, draws people's attention to his own inefficiency.
- Those base men who speak of the secret faults of others destroy themselves like serpents that stray onto ant hills.
- There is no one in this world whose family or lineage does not suffer from some shortcomings or defects.

Fear

- As soon as the fear approaches near, attack and destroy it.

- A thing may be dreaded as long as it has not overtaken you, but once it has come upon you, try to get rid of it without hesitation.

Flattery

- We should always speak what would please the man of whom we expect a favour, like a hunter who sings sweetly when he desires to shoot a deer.
- A sweet talker can convert even an enemy into a friend.
- Like many fruits which look good from the outside are not sweet, similarly, people who talk sweet can be dangerous and untrustworthy. People, who flatter you in front of you and criticise you behind your back, are not fit to be your friends. They are like poison in milk. One should always be wary of them and get rid of them at the earliest.
- All creatures are pleased by loving words. Therefore, we should address words that are pleasing to all, for there is no lack of sweet words.

Food

- A man should never reject food just because it is not tasty. He should gladly accept whatever food he gets, be it simple or fit for royals.

- Water, sugarcane, milk, vegetables, beetle leaf, fruits and medicines have been classified as most pure substances in the scriptures. So, you can perform religious rites even after you have consumed them. There is no bar to their eating.
- It is the stomach which controls your fitness. It is, therefore, essential to keep digestion in order. In case of indigestion, water acts as a medicine. So, drink a lot of water, but do so before eating or after digestion of the food. If water is taken immediately after taking food, it acts like a slow poison and deteriorates the body.
- The addition of ghee (fat) in the food provides maximum strength and nourishment. When compared to wheat, its flour provides ten times more nourishment; milk contains ten times more nourishment than flour; meat provides eight times more nourishment than milk; but ghee is the best. Its regular intake provides immense strength and nourishment. So, it must be consumed in the right measure in the diet.
- A person, who observes silence for a year while eating food, enjoys the pleasures of heaven for millions of years to come.

Fools

- A foolish person is like an animal with two legs. He can neither differentiate between right and wrong nor can he be taught anything. So, leave the company of such a person at the earliest.

- If a fool considers a diamond to be an ordinary stone, the diamond cannot be blamed for this, for it will still remain a diamond. A cruel person may go to any extent in criticising and humiliating a talented person, yet his qualities remain as they are, their importance is never diminished.
- A fool acts foul with even those who do good for him or her.
- Foolish and ignorant people are subjected to jeering. Amongst the learned people, they are like a crow amongst swans.
- An ignorant person is neither able to express his ideas nor can he accept ideas of wisdom from others.
- Do not keep company with a fool for as we can see he is a two-legged beast. Like an unseen thorn, he pierces the heart with his sharp words.
- There are three gems upon this earth—food, water, and pleasing words. Fools consider pieces of rocks as gems.
- A fool's strength may be immense but it is useless, as in the absence of intelligence, he will never be able to use it effectively.

Friendship

- There is some self-interest behind every friendship. There is no friendship without self-interest. This is a bitter truth.
- Never make friends with people who are above or below you in status. Such friendship will never give you any happiness.
- A friend is a true friend if he maintains affectionate relations even during the period of your distress.
- He who befriends a man whose conduct is vicious, whose vision impure, and who is notoriously crooked, is rapidly ruined.
- For a person going abroad, education is his true friend and for the family, a loyal wife is a true friend. For a sick person, his medicine is a true friend.
- A man's true well-wisher is the one who extends you support in sickness, famine, crisis, and invasion and after death takes part in your cremation. A true friend is one who shares both happiness and sorrow.
- It is useless to expect support or affection from a friend, who is deceitful and treacherous. Befriend only a person who is able and trustworthy.
- It is always best to make friends with good people. Because, as water becomes milk by mixing with the

milk, same we become good by making friends with good people.

- Strength comes from the collection of friends.
- Just as a mirror reflects a man's face, his personality is reflected in his choice of friends. One must always be careful in forming friendships and acquaintances, for one's friends, are in a way, an extension of one's inner inclinations and tendencies.
- Whoever helps you in times of illness, misfortune, famines, and invasion is your true brother in the real sense.
- The company of milk makes even water as good as milk. Silver becomes gold when mixed with gold.
- A friend is a friend in an emergency.
- In the case when a friend turns enemy, he can cause major damage to you because he is aware of your personal secrets.
- It is better to be without a friend than have a friend who is unreliable, cunning and evil because such a friend can ruin you anytime.

❑

G

Gentlemen

- A person, who is satisfied with the available means and devotes himself to worshipping God regularly, is a gentleman. Contrary to this, a greedy, discontented and atheist person is evil.
- A person who considers others' women as mothers, others' wealth as dirt and treats others as equals, is a saint-gentleman. That is, a person with noble character, tolerance, contentment, generosity and compassion is a true gentleman.
- A gentleman is bestowed with virtues. He has qualities like faith in religion, sweet nature, willingness to donate, affability, respect for gurus, maturity, politeness, generosity, knowledge of scriptures, good taste and pleasant nature. Against this, a person without these qualities is an evil person.

- One can learn a lot in the company of gentlemen. On the contrary, the company of evil men will only lead to misdeeds and crimes.
- The company of gentlemen and qualified persons raises the level of common people. Therefore, people should seek the company of saintly persons.
- A saint or gentleman has a strange nature. While most people commit numerous sinful acts to attain wealth, wealth for a gentleman is like a blade of grass. Wealth has no value in his eyes. He may become extremely wealthy, yet he does not display any arrogance or commit any sins. There is no change in his humility. Physical pleasure or change in status does not affect his behaviour.

Goals

- One who can't determine his goals; cannot win.

God

- God dwells not in the wooden, stone or earthen idols. His abode is in our feeling and thoughts. It is only through the feelings that we deem God existing in these idols.
- God is not present in idols. Your feelings are your God. The soul is your temple.

- At the time of birth of the child itself, God takes care of his food. Whatever he is destined to get, nobody can snatch it from him. So, instead of hoarding food and amassing wealth, focus on being righteous.
- No one has control over love and faith. Wherever this mind goes, God is visible there.
- If a man develops an affectionate attachment with God, He is always close by. So, man should tie affectionate bonding with God through worship.
- Only God is a powerful and extremely kindhearted ruler of all three worlds and omnipresent.
- Age, action, wealth, education and death are decided and controlled by God; nobody can alter them; yet man should keep making efforts.
- Eyes full of love, head bowed in reverence, helping hands, feet walking on the path of justice and a tongue-speaking truth are God's favourite things.

Greed

- Do not expect truthful conduct from a person who is greedy for money. To earn money, he will resort to telling any kind of lies.
- If a man is greedy, he need not worry about his enemies, because greed is his biggest enemy, which leads him towards ruin.

- People having greed and vested interests never experience true happiness during their lifetime. They are always under mental stress and remain disturbed.

Growth

- Growth and decay are always in one's own hands.

Guest

- A guest is important only if his stay is short. If he extends his stay shamelessly, it leads to graceless outcomes.
- As a prostitute leaves a poor man, the subjects leave a defeated king and birds leave a dead tree, likewise, a guest must quickly leave after having and praising the food offered to him.
- A guest coming from a distant place, a tired traveller and a refugee are like gods. So, a man should first feed them their fill and then eat himself.

Guru

- A guru who shows his disciple the path of righteousness leaves a huge debt. It cannot be paid back as none of the physical objects is so precious.
- With the blessings of the guru alone, a man breaks free from the arena of affection and wealth and becomes capable to come face-to-face with the Lord.

- In fact, the guru acts like a bridge between the God and devotee.
- A person, who preaches divine knowledge and gives the right direction to society is a guru. Such a guru must always be revered.
- A person, who forsakes his guru, is like that immoral woman who is humiliated in society.
- Any person, who leaves his guru's ashram and wanders around to gain knowledge, even if he gains knowledge from anywhere, becomes a laughing stock in the gathering of scholars. Such a person, despite being knowledgeable, is not respected in society.

❑

Habits

- A bad habit is developed through overindulgence and a good habit is developed through chastisement.
- Those who wear dirty clothes, whose teeth are dirty, who overeat, who use offensive language and who sleep during sunrise or sunset, lose their grace, health and beauty and even God deserts them.

Happiness

- Who realizes all the happiness he desires? Everything is in the hands of God. Therefore, one should learn contentment.
- Righteous conduct is the root of happiness.
- A person, whose son is obedient, whose wife is loyal, who is well-mannered and fully satisfied with his hard-earned income, enjoys the bliss of heaven in his lifetime.

- A man is happy if he and his family members are filled with happiness.
- Having a pious and loyal wife, having a son and daughter-in-law with good qualities and having adequate wealth to meet the needs, are the three important features for a man to lead a happy life.
- A person can feel happiness and peace only in the company of a virtuous son, loyal wife and gentleman.
- He who gives up shyness in monetary dealings, acquiring knowledge, eating and business, becomes happy.
- Being happy doesn't mean everything is perfect, rather it means that you have learned to live life despite every sorrow.

Handling

- The fire, the water, the woman, the fool, the snake and the royal family: while these are useful for a man but maybe ruinous for him if he is careless in dealing with them. So, they must be dealt with caution.
- Religion, medicines, wealth, paddy and the guru's orders must be carefully handled.

Hermit

- For a recluse, truth is like mother, knowledge is like father, religion is like a brother, compassion is like a sister, peace is like wife and forgiveness is like son. In reality, in this mortal world, they are true relations/ friends. That is why even a recluse is not alone.

- The greatness of a hermit lies in his ability to forgive.
- As a hermit purifies himself in the fire of religious austerity and earns holy virtues, a student, while treading on a tortuous path, attains invaluable wealth like education.

Honesty

- A person should not be too honest. Straight trees are cut first and honest people are screwed first.
- To test the purity of gold, it is heated at high temperature; it is tapped, hammered and cut to give it the glitter. Similarly, an honest person is tested for purity by his acts of charity, noble deeds, virtuosity, sacrifice and good conduct. Any person, who possesses all these qualities glitters like gold.

House

- A house is like a crematorium where Brahmins are not respected, whose residents are averse to charity, where study and reading of the Vedas are not practised, and where yajnas are not performed. Such an abode is filled with ignorance, poverty, sickness, sorrows and difficulties. The people residing in such a house are like corpses.

- Where there is all-round happiness and pleasure, the wife has a sweet nature and is loyal, the children are intelligent and well educated; where sufficient funds are available, the servants are obedient and loyal; where the guests are appropriately welcomed and looked after, God's worship is practised and saints are welcomed—such a home is filled with happiness.

Humility

- The root of humility is in the service of the seniors—elderly or old persons. When one renders honest service to elders, one learns the worth of humility.
- It is better to have no king than a king who doesn't know humility.

❑

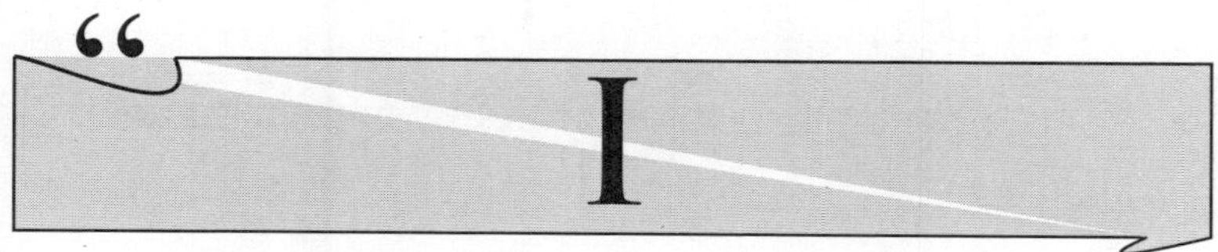

Intelligent Men

- Intelligent persons detect their benefits even amidst a crisis.
- A person is intelligent when he speaks at the right time, shows heroism according to his strength and displays anger as per his capacity. If a man digresses from the topic of discussion, does not know his strength and gets angry unnecessarily, he is considered an intelligent fool.
- If an intelligent person gains a little knowledge, he is able to expand it further.
- Only at the right time, do intelligent people take up the tasks suited to that time. Against this, people who undertake tasks unmindful of the time, fail.
- An intelligent man can effectively use his strength. His strength might be little, yet he can use it well.

- Even intelligent and wise men are ruined after some time if they remain in the company of immoral, sinful, wicked or cruel persons. Such persons are like a coal mine where everything turns black. Avoid friendship with such persons.
- It is more important to be intelligent rather than being strong.

❑

Jealousy

- Always sow a seed of dissension between the people nursing jealousy for you.
- A gentleman is never jealous of others' grandeur, opulence, progress and happiness, rather he is satisfied with his own meagre means.

Judgement

- Don't judge the future of a person based on his present conditions, because time has the power to change black coal to a shiny diamond.
- You can guess the origin of a person through his behaviour, his native place via his tone, and his food intake by looking at the size of his belly.
- By observing a man's personality, an intelligent person can judge his good and bad qualities.

Judiciary

- The lack of a proper penal code enhances unlawful activities in the state.
- A culprit should be punished by the judge according to the intensity of the crime committed by him and not out of any personal grudge.

❑

Kindness

- If a person is kind to others, he does not require to don the cloth of a recluse or hermit to gain knowledge and attain salvation. What remains rare for ascetics despite hundreds of years of self-penance, is the knowledge and salvation that can be realized easily by being kind to mankind.

King

- The king who goes on the illegal path and doesn't care about the pains and problems of his citizens, will be destroyed by his own selfishness. Similarly, a man who does not care about his society, dies.
- It is the duty of a king to know the difficulties being faced by his people; how his officers behave with the people and what actions they are taking for their welfare. So, to get first-hand information, he should travel incognito.

- The king has to bear for the sins committed by his subjects.
- It is the duty of the king to eliminate all kinds of sins in his kingdom; he should not allow arbitrariness and evil to spread in his territory. This will ensure that the people in his kingdom lead a fearless life and the king shall reap its rewards.
- True knowledge helps the King discharge his duties more efficiently.
- A king and a gentleman should use their wealth for welfare and charity, instead of amassing it.
- If a king is religious and talented, his subjects would also be religious and talented. If he is a sinner, his subjects would also behave accordingly; because the subjects follow the king.
- Without good assistants, a king can take no right decisions.
- Proximity to a king and guru makes a person arrogant and he becomes blemished; whereas staying away from them leads to neglect.
- An able king can train his assistant to become an efficient ruler and then he can rule efficiently.
- When the king becomes stronger and controls the nation, then the petty thieves, terrorists and traitors feel the heat and complain of intolerance in the society.

- A king's strength lies in his arms, with which he destroys his enemy.
- A king should choose only a well-learned and of strong character person as his minister. A minister should have an open mind and unfinishable loyalty to his king.
- The king shall lose no time when the opportunity waited for arrives.
- It is better to be without a king than to have a bad one.

Knowledge

- Knowledge is lost without putting it into practice; a man is lost due to ignorance; an army is lost without a commander; and a woman is lost without a husband.
- Knowledge is like a holy kamandal and tree that bears fruit in every season. In unknown territories, it provides protection and brings you rewards.
- One whose knowledge is confined to books and whose wealth is in the possession of others can use neither knowledge nor wealth when the need for them arises.
- Infatuation is the biggest disease, greed is the worst enemy of an individual, anger is the endless fire, and among all possessions, knowledge is supreme.

- Give only adequate knowledge to a person that he could understand because on not closing the tap after filling a bucket with water, the water gets wasted.
- This world is filled with immense knowledge. The human soul, even after taking hundreds of births, cannot acquire all the knowledge. But as the swan can drink only milk and leave the water, a person should extract essential elements from numerous scriptures and other treatises.
- One must imbibe knowledge from wherever one can.
- If knowledge is not used, it is forgotten; the neglect of a person makes him inactive; without the commander, the army dissipates; and without the husband, the wife is ruined.
- No thief can steal knowledge.

❑

Laziness

- The lazy have neither present nor future.
- The lazy can't protect even the advantage already received.
- Laziness and irregular practices corrupt the intelligence of scholars and ruin their knowledge.

Learned Man

- A learned man is honoured by the people. A learned man commands respect everywhere for his learning. Indeed, learning is honoured everywhere.
- A person, who even after studying religious scriptures like the Vedas, remains ignorant of the essential elements, does not have knowledge of the Soul and God and remains devoid of knowledge of his spiritual self. He is like a ladle, which stirs the juicy curry but remains unaware of its taste and usefulness; such knowledge is nothing but meaningless.

- A hesitant professional engaged in trade, teaching, eatery and money-lending is sure to face a lot of problems and difficulties.

Life

- Life is 10% what happens to you and 90% how you react to it. The difference between a successful person and others is not a lack of strength or knowledge, but rather it is a lack of willpower to apply the knowledge and strength.
- Life's every moment, hour and day are important. So, man must use it purposefully.
- Sometimes you have to suffer in life, not because you were bad but because you didn't realize where to stop being good.
- A long life with sorrows and sins is very painful. Such a life has no meaning. Against this, if a man's life is filled with good deeds, it is like pleasure despite its length. Whatever his age, a man should do good deeds. His welfare rests on them.
- A hungry stomach, empty pocket and false love teach a man many lessons in life.
- Wealth, property, friendship, pleasure and power can be obtained repeatedly, but the human form is attained only once. Once it is annihilated, it is impossible to attain it again. So, a man should perform good

deeds and use them for worthy causes. Only the life of people, who perform good deeds every day, is a success.

- A person who has not earned sufficient money in his life, who does not worship God to free himself from this worldly bond and who has never copulated, does not benefit this world or set right his other world.

Lion

- The one excellent thing that can be learned from a lion is that, whatever a man intends to do, should be done by him with a whole-hearted and strenuous effort.
- There is no official ceremony held to declare the lion the king of the forest. He himself becomes the king of the forest through his own attributes and heroism.
- The lion is gifted with an important quality of sincere courage, which a man should imbibe. If a man took responsibility for a work, he should fulfil it with sincerity and courage. However, before taking up the responsibility, he should introspect about his strengths and weaknesses.

Love

- Rain falling on an ocean is meaningless, feeding a well-fed person is meaningless, charity to a rich person is meaningless and lighting a lamp in daylight is meaningless. Similarly, it is meaningless to love a stone-hearted person.

- The bond of true love binds mutually to great depths. In such a state, even if one is away, the other feels him to be close by.
- Love for others is true love.
- We have to make people soft who are hard, to attract those who are far, and if they do bad to us then considering our aim, we should always love them.
- He who lives in our mind is near though he may actually be far away, he who is not in our heart is far though he may really be nearby.

Lust

- There is no disease so destructive as lust.
- Lust is a man's most powerful enemy. It is such an untreatable disease under the influence of which a man loses his wisdom, while his health deteriorates rapidly.
- There is no end to a man's desires and lust. Fulfilment of one's desire leads to bringing into existence of several others.

❑

Marriage

- Marry a woman who is well-mannered and from a well-bred family. It will enhance the pleasures of married life.

Meditation

- Any man, who sheds conceit and develops a passion for worshipping God in his mind, wherever his mind may wander, can still meditate. If he is able to understand the true relationship between body and soul, he can meditate wherever he may be.

Men

- The gold is tested in four ways—by rubbing, cutting, heating and beating. Similarly, a man is tested by his sacrifice, behaviour, qualities and actions.
- Avoid him who talks sweetly before you but tries to ruin you behind your back, for he is like a pitcher full of poison with milk on top.

- We should not fret about what's in past, nor should we be anxious about the future; men of discernment deal only with the present moment.
- A man is born alone and dies alone, and he experiences the good or bad consequences of his karma alone, and he goes alone to hell or the supreme abode.
- In the forest, only the trees which grow straight are cut and nobody bothers about trees which grow in a haphazard manner. So, a man should not be so simple that people can easily exploit him.
- Desires never let a man live and a man never let desires die.
- A person's face at the age of twenty is the gift of nature. A person's face at the age of thirty is the gift of life's ups and downs. But a person's face at the age of fifty is his own earnings.
- A person does nothing but plays with his own life if he keeps the company of a sharp-tongued woman, makes a sinful friend, or retains a traitorous and selfish servant. Such a person can be consumed by death at any time.
- A man should imbibe the two qualities of patience and contentment. These will ensure that he is at peace with himself and is satisfied.
- A man should never mock a helpless and afflicted person, because tomorrow he may find himself in the same situation.

- A person who keeps demanding his rights is greedy. A person who attaches importance to beauty and external outlook is lustful. Foolish people are by nature not soft-spoken. Contrarily, a frank and truthful person does not have even an iota of cunningness, deceit and craftiness.
- An industrious father, a religious mother, a loyal wife and an intelligent son are all the true well-wishers of a man. In fact, their support leads him towards the righteous path.
- He who is prepared for the future and he who deals cleverly with any situation that may arise are both happy, but the fatalistic man who wholly depends on luck is ruined.
- A man's welfare lies in helping others. Anyone whose heart is filled with benevolence never faces a crisis.
- A person who steals the wealth of saints, who is a consummated adulterator and who has no hesitation in begging for food, such a person may be a Brahmin but is classified as a hangman.

Mercy

- A man who has mercy and compassion for all creatures is religious for sure. He does not require any religious symbol or sign to prove his religiousness.

Mind

- No one can defeat a powerful mind.
- There is no austerity equal to a balanced mind, and there is no happiness equal to contentment; there is no disease like covetousness and no virtue like mercy.
- It is the mind of man alone that is the cause of his bondage or freedom.
- A person mired in bad deeds disgraces not only himself but his family as well.
- The mind is the root cause of all bonds and sorrows.
- It is only the mind which pushes a man towards the sense of sexual enjoyment and leads him towards sins.
- A man under the hypnosis of the mind can never free himself from the cycle of life and death. So, a man should have control over all his weaknesses of the mind. Only then it will be possible for him to improve his life in the other world.

Mistakes

- Learn from the mistakes of others. You can't live long enough to make them all yourselves.

Mother

- In any case, the mother should be fed first.

- Man has five mothers—the king's wife, guru's wife, friend's wife, wife's mother and his mother; he should extend due respect to them all. Anyone, who shows evil intent against them or disrespects them, suffers in hell.

Morality

- Moral excellence is an ornament for personal beauty; righteous conduct, high birth; success for learning; and proper spending for wealth.

❑

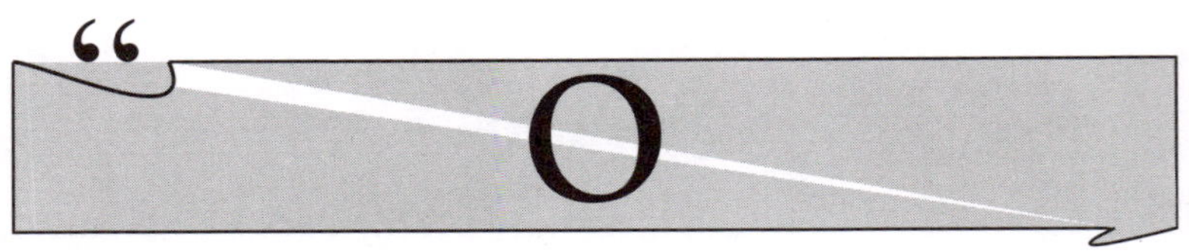

Old Age

- Walking lost in thought for long periods, keeping horses tied to their holders, denying women sexual pleasures and drying clothes in sun for very long are signs of the arrival of old age. So, avoid them.

Ostentation

- The elegance of the hand is enhanced, not by wearing jewellery, but by charity; the body is cleansed, not by applying sandalwood paste, but by bathing; mental contentment rests, not in food, but in honour; and salvation is attained, not by applying vermilion or wearing saffron clothes, but by knowledge. Similarly, the mind attains peace, not by superficial ostentation or indulging in sexual lust, but by becoming pure.
- Inner satisfaction comes from helping others, being kind, being virtuous and with a donation, and not by ostentation.

❑

P

People Required

- Meditation, prayer and learning of a lesson should be done alone; the involvement of more persons will only create obstacles. Contrarily, studies are better done by two persons together; more than two persons will indulge in wasteful talk. For singing, three persons are adequate; whereas for travel, four persons are appropriate. For farming are required five persons and for war, the largest number of persons are required.

Place

- A man shouldn't live in a place where people are not afraid of the law, are shameless, and there is no clever man; where people lack in kindness, and where no creativity or art exists.
- A place where a man does not have respect, a source of income, suitable well-wishing friends and

relations, and facilities for learning, such a place is the most unsuitable. It should be abandoned without any further delay

- A place which lacks five basic conveniences, i.e., Brahmins to perform religious ceremonies, a just king, prosperous traders, flowing rivers and proper medical facilities, is totally unsuitable for an intelligent person. It should be abandoned immediately.
- A place where people do not have faith in this or the next world, where people do not believe in the existence of God, where people do not believe in the welfare of others or charity, an intelligent person should never consider settling there.
- A state in which sins and sinners abound, instead of staying there, it is better to stay in an isolated place.
- In a kingdom, where the king is evil, irreligious and a sinner, people can never live there in peace. People should choose to reside only in a kingdom where the king is righteous.
- In a foreign place, a man should adapt himself according to the situation and his income. Like the beetle that normally lives on the lily leaves and is used to being immersed in the juice from its pollen, but in a foreign place, it has to be satisfied with the odourless and tasteless juice of the thorny bush. Likewise, in a foreign place, a man should be satisfied with the

available food. It will help him change favourably as per that place.

Poison

- Poison is poison in all circumstances.
- If it were possible to extract nectar from poison, it would be appropriate to consume it without any hesitation. Similarly, you must accept gold extracted from impure metals, learning from a common man and a cultured woman from a low caste without delay.

Policy

- Home Policy must relate to the interior matters of the state.
- Foreign Policy relates to dealing with foreign countries.

Poverty and Poor Person

- A poor man should be patient. This will help him endure the difficulties of his poverty, within his limited resources. If he kept his lowly clothes neat and clean, he would be able to improve his appearance. If he ate frugal food hot, it would be tasty.
- A person without wealth is not poor, but a person without wisdom and education is truly poor.

- A wealthy fool cannot earn respect for himself. However, a poor scholar can attain a respectable place in society.
- On becoming poor, a person may be mocked often: such a situation is extremely stressful and can cause mental tension. Nobody is ready to support a poor man.
- If some rich person turned poor, even the dear ones desert him. His wife, son, friends, and other relations leave him one after another.
- In meetings and seminars, a poor person is always insulted. So, for him, such places are like poison.

Power

- The world's biggest power is a woman's youth and beauty.
- People express their existence through some power: a Brahmin (scholar) expresses his existence through the depth of his knowledge, a king through the might of his army, a businessman through the aura of his wealth and a servant through his servility expresses his existence. A person is completely useless without some form of power.
- Helplessness keeps a man and his character from going astray.

- Lack of power compels a man to turn celibate; lack of wealth makes a man become saintly; lack of health makes a person start worshipping God; lack of youth makes a woman become loyal to her husband.

Practice

- We are what we repeatedly do. Excellence is not an act, but a habit.
- It is only through constant practice that knowledge can be retained.
- Without practice, even scholars cannot recite manuscripts properly and will be mocked. For them, this insult will be more painful than death. So, for a scholar, who does not practice regularly, the text is like poison.

Problems

- If one has the dedication to find a clue to solve a problem, no problem remains difficult.
- When one finds a problem arising in the work, one should examine all the aspects of it minutely to find the fault and remove it.
- The Gayatri Mantra, of all the mantras (sacred hymn), is the supreme recitation and is the one that fulfils all the desires. Recite it every day to eliminate all obstructions from life.

Purity

- Water stored in the depths of the earth, a loyal woman, a welfare-oriented king and a content Brahmin: these four are the purest.
- If a man's mind were filled with sins and impurities, taking several dips in holy places could not purify his soul.

❑

Qualities

- The qualities that come from birth cannot be changed. If you pour the milk on the neem tree, neem will remain neem only. It will not become jaggery.
- Even though the crow is sitting on the tallest building, it could not be called a Garuda. Similarly, a person's honour is determined by his qualities, not by his height, position or wealth.
- Good characteristics are carried forward from the previous birth. Being benevolent, educated, restrained, and virtuous are some of the good traits that are carried forward from several previous births. Life must be made purposeful by making use of them.
- Sometimes, even one good quality overrides many bad qualities.
- Generosity, pleasing address, courage and propriety of conduct are not acquired but are inbred qualities.

- Like a sandalwood tree does not become poisonous even though poisonous snakes rest on it, and like the flower, which grows in the soil, does not carry its smell, a gentleman in the company of evil people, does not shed his righteousness and good qualities.
- The fragrance of flowers spreads only in the direction of the wind. But the goodness of a person spreads in all directions.
- Instead of the full moon, the waning moon of the following day is worshipped. Similarly, a poor person of a lower caste possessing good qualities is treated respectfully.
- The more you subject to pressure the sugarcane, oilseeds, a worker, woman, gold, earth, sandalwood, curd and betel leaf the more qualities they develop.
- God has definitely given some quality or the other to every living thing. So, the qualities of even a foolish person or lowly animal should also be accepted without any hesitation or shame.
- A great person possesses four qualities of charity, courteous speech, faith in religion and welcoming to scholars. He is ever ready to donate; his speech is sweet at all times; his psyche is fully devoted to God and he always respects scholars.
- There is no greater devotion than peace, greater happiness than contentment and greater sickness than greed.

- The capacity to carry the load despite being bone-tired, being undaunted by the vagaries of weather and getting satisfied in all the conditions—these are qualities to be learned from the donkey.
- Charity is an effective means of alleviating poverty. Modesty eliminates degradation and hardships. Knowledge puts an end to stupidity and ignorance, whereas courtesy destroys fear. So, for living peacefully, a man should develop and imbibe all these four qualities.
- Even if one has a single bad quality, it shall nullify all his other good qualities.
- A wise, clever, radiant and strong person can overcome even the most difficult problems. Superiority is not in size but inherent in these four qualities.
- The stork has the quality of patient concentration. A stork focuses its sight on its prey patiently and expels all other thoughts from its mind; likewise, an intelligent and wise person should control all his senses, focus himself patiently and complete his work.
- Even the symbol of foolishness, the donkey has three qualities. Toiling tirelessly, not being bothered by hot or cold weather, being patient and contented—the presence of these qualities can make a man's life worthwhile.

- An intelligent and wise person ought to imbibe four qualities from the cock. Getting up at a fixed time; being ever ready for a fight; sharing fairly with friends and sexually satisfying its hen. Like the cock rises early and attends to its chores, similarly, a man should also rise early and attend to his chores faithfully.
- The crow is gifted with five qualities—performing sex in private; being wicked and adamant; having nature to store; never being lazy and never trusting anyone: all of which a man should imbibe.
- Having a large appetite, being satisfied with less in adversity, having a sound sleep, remaining alert even while sleeping, and facing the enemy with loyalty and courage—the dog has these six qualities. These six qualities are superlative for a man.
- Beauty is enhanced by good qualities.
- If you are very beautiful and youthful but without any qualities, you will face insult and disregard.

❑

R

Relations

- Relations of affection and attraction are appropriate only with a person of your status.
- Man's relations are truly his supporters. If he abandons them and rushes towards others, he is ruined very soon.

Religion

- Wealth, youth and life can be destroyed one by one. However, religion is indestructible, immortal and eternal; nobody can destroy it.
- The practice of religion dispels all sorrows of a man, in this as well as the other world.
- A man can pray before idols made from any material, but it is more necessary to have true dedication and reverence. In fact, it is only on account of this faith that God resides in his heart and he feels the

presence of God in inanimate objects and attains salvation.

- A person can reap the benefits of pleasing God if he performs all religious ceremonies himself. Activities like making the flower garland and placing it on the idol himself, applying the self-made sandalwood paste and reciting the self-written hymns in the praise of God and others will enable him to obtain divine grace. In contrast, if he gets all these ceremonies done through a servant, the benefits will accrue to the servant. So, a person should perform all religious ceremonies himself.
- Any person, who gives up his religion and is attracted towards another religion, in spite of being affluent, is ruined. So, a man should never be indifferent to his own religion.
- A religion which protects from sins, falsehood and derogatory acts is a true religion.
- A person should enjoy all the worldly pleasures in this world; but at the same time, undertake religious activities to try and improve his life in the other world.
- Anyone who performs religious activities and observes his duties deserves to be called a true human.

- Never accept a religion which is bereft of compassion; never accept a person as a guru who is not a scholar; never take an extremely short-tempered woman as a wife. Similarly, never have high hopes for children who lack affection; and never consider those people dear and trustworthy who does not value friendship.
- Man has the good fortune of earning blessings by performing religious acts. So, perform them and be blessed. This will ensure the shaping of your future in this and the other world.

Reputation

- If an evil person chases away a beggar, it makes no difference to the beggar, who goes and gets alms from another house. But the person loses his reputation forever.

Responsibilities

- Those who run away from their responsibilities are never able to nurture their dependents properly.
- The cowards don't care for their work or duties.
- Feeling for others' sorrow and being ever ready to help others are man's true duties.
- Praying to God and visiting religious places are not the only duties of a man, serving others and humanity are among his true duties.

Respect

- I have a lot of respect for myself. I don't see myself as somebody who needs to be loved by anyone else.
- You can't respect yourself if you don't respect others.
- Respect yourself. You were born that way.
- Respect yourself, because you are worth it.
- When compared to fame, the radiance of all jewellery of the world is inferior.
- The fire, the guru, the Brahmin (scholar), the cow, the girl, the aged and the child must be respected and honoured. Therefore, they must never be touched with your feet.
- What is respect? It is the knowledge that your own dignity is more important than any other consideration.
- I possess command over the Sanskrit language, yet I yearn to learn the other superior languages of the world because this will make me get respect in the world.
- Respect yourself, and you will win the respect of others.
- A person who respects himself will respect others. A person who doesn't respect himself has no one to blame but himself.

- A person praised by the world truly deserves the respect.

Reward

- Feeding a hungry person and offering water to a thirsty person is most holistically rewarding.

❑

Sacrifice

- If you can protect your village or society by relinquishing or sacrificing one family, it is entirely appropriate.

Salvation

- If a man wanted to release from the cycle of life-death and attain salvation, he should completely abandon perversions like sex, anger, greed, allurement and arrogance. These perversions are like poison for any man.
- God provides the soul with a human life only for its salvation. But a man gets attracted towards weaknesses like sex, anger, greed, addiction, attachment and the like and goes astray from his aim.
- A person should imbibe qualities like forgiveness, simplicity, patience, politeness, honesty, generosity,

welfare, mercy, truth, love and purity. This enables him to be free of all sinful acts and attain salvation.

Saving

- Any person who saves for hard times or crises is an intelligent person. All efforts must be made to protect such savings.
- A woman is like your wealth, so she must also be protected. But before all this, a man must ensure his own security, for if he was secure, he would be capable to secure his wealth and woman.
- People must save for the crisis. But a man should never think that he would be able to avert the crisis by his wealth alone. Lakshmi, the goddess of wealth, is mobile and never stationary in any place. While the accumulation of wealth is an indication of intelligence, it does not mean that crisis can be averted by it alone.
- Tiny drops can fill a pot and form a river, small pennies can add to make a man wealthy; you can make a fortune out of small savings.

Scholars

- A scholar is able to look into the inner thinking of others without saying anything. Nothing remains a secret before their intelligence and knowledge.

- A person is a barbarian who feels elated in damaging wells, gardens and temples. A scholar who is unconcerned with the welfare of society and who shirks his social responsibilities is a degenerate.
- Even if the diamond were tied to the feet and glass were adorned on the head, it would not diminish the value of the diamond. Likewise, placing a scholar on a lower seat and a fool on a higher seat would not diminish the status of the scholar.
- A jewel becomes more attractive when it is laid in gold, if it were laid in iron, it would lose its glitter and grace; similarly, a scholar should seek an appropriate place for himself.
- A scholar who uses his knowledge to earn wealth only is useless to society. His existence in society is of no consequence. He will never be known for his intelligence and knowledge in the world.

Secrets

- Never share your secrets with anybody. It will destroy you.
- Never reveal what you have thought upon doing, but by wise council keep it secret being determined to carry it into execution.
- Never share your secrets with someone lacking depth of character.

- A person who exposes others' secrets is degenerated, meddlesome and evil. Such a person initially feels elated by insulting others, but he is later ruined like a snake trapped in an anthill.
- While planning out or implementing any desired work, if you disclose it, its successful conclusion becomes doubtful. So, take care not to disclose it to anyone till its successful conclusion.

Self-Control and Control

- Humbleness is at the root of self-control.
- Control the greedy by money, arrogant by submissiveness, the fool by preaching, and the learned by telling him the reality.
- He who controls his senses has his all wishes fulfilled. He gets wealth and prosperity in every way.
- A person, greedy by nature, can be controlled by allurement alone. An obstinate and arrogant person can be controlled by politeness. If a foolish and brainless person's wishes are fulfilled, he can be easily controlled. To mould an intelligent person, he must be made aware of the facts.

Selfishness

- As a drunkard does not know right or wrong, in the same way, a selfish human will not realize right or wrong.

- A selfish and sinning person is as good as a blind. He never thinks twice about causing hurt to others and fulfilling his selfish interests. For him, there is no difference between evil and good deeds. For him, when compared to his vested interests, everything else is meaningless.
- Until there is water in the pond, the swans stay and build their nests on its bank; but when the pond dries, they break away all the attachments and fly away. A selfish person behaves in the same fashion. Till his vested interest is not fulfilled, he remains with his provider and showers his affection. Once his vested interest is fulfilled, he leaves his provider.
- A stupid, poor and poverty-stricken man has selfish motives, so he does not nurse any feelings of love, affection or sympathy. Therefore, he lives in isolation as everyone stays away from him.

Self-respect

- Never settle for anything less than what you deserve. It is not pride. It is self-respect.
- Self-respect is the foundation of all good character, without which no true greatness can be built.
- We should all be able to take pride in our self-esteem and self-respect, no matter where we come from or how much money we have.

Sex

- A sex-minded person is unmindful of the meaning and importance of purity. Such a person only promotes infidelity.

Showmanship

- The showmanship of strength and influence is like a snake; people are scared of a hissing snake even though it may not be poisonous; likewise, a person without any influence must create influence in society through showmanship.

Skills and Talent

- Skills are called hidden treasures as they save like a mother in a foreign country.
- If a wise person is talented, it is the finest confluence.
- Use your talent for the welfare of not only society but also your family.
- When a talented person gets his rightful place, his talent is approved by society.

Sleep

- The serpent, the king, the tiger, the stinging wasp, the child, the dog owned by other people and the fool: these seven ought not to be awakened from sleep.

Snakes

- Even if a snake is not poisonous, it should pretend to be venomous.

Son

- It is better to have only one son endowed with good qualities than a hundred devoid of them. For the moon though one, dispels the darkness, which the stars, though numerous, do not.
- A true son is one, who always obeys his parents.
- Just like a tree laden with scented flowers spreads fragrance in the whole forest. Similarly, a worthy son brings glory to the whole family, community, and country.
- As a single withered tree, if set aflame, causes a whole forest to burn, so does a rascal son destroy a whole family.
- A true son is obedient, a true father is loving, and a true friend is honest.
- A virtuous son, by his knowledge, wisdom and learning, earns a place of pride for the family in society.

Sorrow

- When one is consumed by the sorrows of life, three things give him relief: offspring, a wife, and the company of the Lord's devotees.

- There are some sorrows in a man's life which are impossible to forget. Losing your wife, an insult by a near and dear one, a burden of debt, serving a wicked master and living a life of poverty with fools. These hardships cause illness and push a man towards his death.

- Happiness or sorrow and ups or downs come and go in everyone's life. So, a man should not feel helpless but face difficulties with courage.

- Residing in a bad or ill-reputed place, serving people of unknown background, eating bad food, having a short-tempered wife, a foolish son or a widowed daughter: these six reasons give a person heart-rending pain.

- A king, a prostitute, Yama (the god of Death), the fire, a smuggler, a child, a beggar and the village's nuisance-creator: these eight do not understand the sorrows and distress of others. They act as per their whims. So, a man should not expect any kindness from them.

- A person who has celebrated every moment, who complains less and who for every small achievement has thanked God; such a person experiences sorrow very rarely.

Soul

- As long as your body is healthy and under control and death is distant, try to save your soul. When death is imminent, what can you do? Save your soul from death as much as possible. Once you lost your body, you cannot get it back.
- Respect the power of your own soul. Learn to listen to its whispers and follow them.
- Religious activities like charity, pilgrimage, praying, worshipping, fasting and attending discourses etc. open the way to heaven; they cleanse the soul, so undertake them while you are hale and hearty, observing the proper practices, else there will be nothing left after death.
- It is only after undergoing hardships of several births that the soul is fortunate to be born in the human form. So, instead of wasting it on physical pleasures, it should be used for attaining salvation.
- Refine your soul with knowledge.

Spirituality

- Happiness and peace are attained by those who are satisfied by the nectar of spiritual tranquillity, they are not attained by greedy persons restlessly moving here and there.

- Purity of speech, of the mind, of the senses, and of a compassionate heart are needed by one who desires to rise to the divine platform.
- By reciting the sacred mantra of 'Om', a man can easily secure divine knowledge.

Students

- A student who wishes to attain knowledge while being attached to the allurement/wealth and pleasures of life can never succeed in his mission.
- A student, who desires pleasure, should shun the idea of getting an education. The paths to enjoying the physical pleasure and getting an education don't cross each other. It is difficult to attain both simultaneously.
- A student, who can put his learning into practice, can benefit from it in life.

Success

- It's not whether you get knocked down; it's whether you get up.
- Success consists of going from failure to failure without a loss of enthusiasm.
- A person cannot get success in any task if he lacks faith in it. He can be successful in a task which is done with mental dedication and sacrifice.

- Without full involvement, you cannot attain success in any task.
- Success in the project is achieved only when prior deliberations are held as closely guarded secrets.
- Every new beginning is a little scary but remember success is seen only near difficulties.
- The one who depends on luck never achieves success in his/her assignments.
- A wise person should never discuss with others his knowledge of an unfailing medicine, his religious customs, his domestic problems, his relations with a woman, bad food and abusive discussions. He should keep such things to himself. If he discusses such things with others, his being a scholar is meaningless.

❑

T

Tasks

- The greatest tasks can be completed by completing smaller tasks first. It is similar to a thick rope which is used to tie wild elephants in anger. The thick rope gains its strength from several small threads tied together.
- A student, employee, traveller, hungry person, scared person, storekeeper and doorman can only complete their tasks while remaining awake.
- Any task undertaken with complete dedication never fails to reward.

Testing

- Test a servant while in the discharge of his duty, a relative in difficulty, a friend in adversity, and a wife in misfortune.
- Servants are tested by fulfilment of their responsibilities, friends are tested in times of crisis,

relations are tested in times of sorrow or incurable sickness and a woman is tested when you have no money.

Time

- Time perfects men, as well as destroy them. Time is in nobody's hands. Nobody is a friend or enemy to none. Time makes everyone friends and enemies.
- Time or death is most powerful. It is so powerful that it can destruct anything in this universe in no time. Even when universal destruction causes it to disappear underwater, time will still be ticking. The cycle of time is perpetually in motion.
- Time devours the beings and destroys creation. It remains active even when the human beings are asleep. No one can check its incessant flow.
- You can't stop time but not wasting your time is under your control.
- A man should focus only on the present. If he improves his present, his future would automatically be bright.
- The past never returns, the events which have happened cannot be changed. So, crying over them repeatedly does not help.
- Have a relationship with a good person rather than with good times. A good man can bring good times but good times cannot bring a good man.

Tit for Tat

- If a person behaves with you like a gentleman, you must reciprocate accordingly. However, if a person intends to harm you, he should be paid back in the same coin.

Too Much

- Too much beauty got Sita kidnapped, too much ego got Ravana killed and too much charity got Raja Bali in deep trouble. So too much of anything is bad. One should refrain from 'too much'.
- Excess of anything or any action is harmful.

Truth

- Nothing is inaccessible or unachievable for those who are endowed with the wealth of truth.
- This world survives on truth alone. The glow of truth is illuminated in the form of the sun in the sky.
- You can take control of a greedy person by paying money. But if you want to control a good person, then you have to tell the truth.
- No devotion is greater than truth. The blaze of truth eliminates all perversions of the body. Therefore, there is no need for a truthful person to undertake devotional penance.

- The earth is supported by the power of truth, it is the power of truth that makes the sun shines and the winds blow, indeed all things rest upon truth.

❑

Unity

- Like a group of hyenas can fight a lion, a roof made of a bundle of straws stops water, similarly, if many weak persons unite, they can face even the mightiest person.

❑

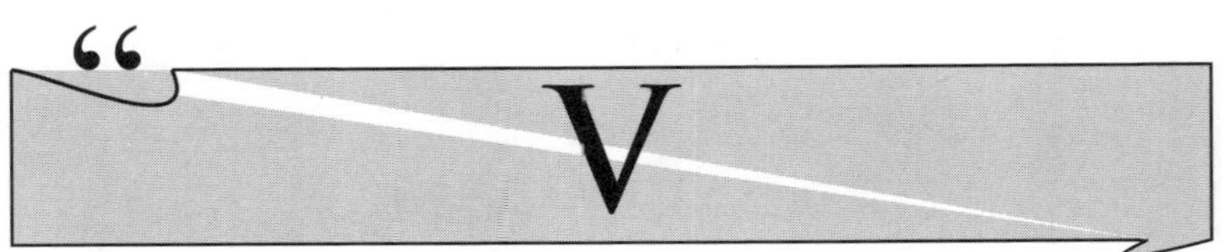

Value

- Even if a gem is placed on the foot and a mirror on the head, still, the gem will not lose its value.
- It is a person's point of view which enhances or depreciates the value of a thing. It appears to him as he wishes to see it.

Varnas

- The Vedas specify four classes of people. They have been classified based on their profession rather than on their descent or caste. The Vaishya (trader) is a person engaged in conventional activities like husbandry, farming and business; if a person born in a Brahmin family undertook these activities, he should also be considered a Vaishya.
- A person engaged in the businesses of lac, oil, blue, dyeing colours, honey, ghee, liquor and meat, is called a Shudra (a low caste). If a person born as a Brahmin,

Kshatriya, or Vaishya undertakes these jobs, he should also be considered a Shudra.

- It is not enough to be born into an upper caste to attain greatness. It is necessary for a man to be tolerant, patient, learned and welfare-minded.

Vedic Learning

- Religious scriptures list four valours—Dharma (religion), Artha (finance), Kama (sex) and Moksha (salvation). Of these, finance and sex have been called the valours of this world, while religion and salvation have been called the valours of the other world. All four of these provide purpose to human life. Without them, life is a waste. So, a man should try to achieve at least one valour.

- Vedic knowledge can drive a man's sin-filled mind towards righteousness. Through its influence, even an ordinary man can attain superiority. The power of Vedic knowledge enables the saints to undertake the welfare of the world and reach heaven after death.

- If the study of the holy texts is not possible for men, then they should listen to its recitation. This will enable them to understand the Vedic knowledge in greater depth.

- The Vedas and other holy scriptures were created by and for intelligent and wise people. They are beneficial only for people who have the ability to think and understand. Fools cannot benefit from them.

Virtues

- Virtues enhance the beauty of the form; good manners enhance the glory of the family; perfection enhances the value of education and enjoyment enhances the pleasure of wealth.
- If a man born into a high-class family with virtuous qualities becomes poor, his politeness, humility and morality do not disappear. He behaves gracefully even in a crisis.

❑

Weakness

- Our problems and pains should not be shared with others. Because people make fun of our weaknesses, laugh at them and take advantage of them.

Wealth

- Give your wealth only to the worthy and never to others. The water of the sea received by the clouds is always sweet.
- Excessive wealth not only corrupts a man's mind but also makes him greedy and selfish.
- If someone were short of knowledge or wisdom but had unlimited wealth, he would be respected in society. In contrast, a poor but knowledgeable, intelligent and wise person would be looked down upon.
- For tough times, one must save money.

- Wealth earned by sinning and malpractice lasts at the most for ten years. In the eleventh year, he loses all this wealth with interest. Against this, wealth earned through hard work and honesty is retained lifelong and keeps growing

- Intoxication of wealth is so powerful that on attaining it even a sensible and learned person turns arrogant. The greed for it places a man in difficulties again and again.

- If the still water in a pond is not changed at regular intervals, it rots and becomes useless. In order to retain its usefulness, it should run continuously. Similarly, the amassed wealth must be circulated by charity. This not only earns esteem for a man in this world but also opens doors for ensuring happiness in the other world.

- If a man has wealth in old age, he does not have to be dependent on others for food. So, to avert this pathetic state, a man should save wealth for old age.

- If wealth is only amassed and not used, it loses its importance.

- Accumulated wealth is saved by spending just as incoming fresh water is saved by letting out stagnant water.

- The wealth earned by unjust means will perish for sure.
- The power of wealth is so great that even unfamiliar persons develop an affinity, whereas poverty drives away relations. The paucity of wealth leaves you alone in adversity. It is only wealth which gains man the highest respect in society.
- If a man becomes rich, even strangers would try to be acquaintances; his wife, son, friends and relations also express affection and become personal.
- Sinfully acquired wealth may remain for ten years; in the eleventh year, it disappears even with the original stock.
- Satisfaction is the greatest wealth.
- Wealth is important and useful only if it serves, not one person, but the whole society. Wealth amassed for the use of one person is like the virtuous woman of a noble family, who gives pleasure to him and none else. So, her existence does not make any difference to society.
- Wealth obtained by sinful acts or by causing distress to others becomes cursed and ruins a man. Such wealth causes even gentlemen to take the path of sin. One must avoid such wealth otherwise he would be ruined along with his family in the distant future.

Wicked People

- Wicked ones are like fire. They don't leave unhurt even their well-wishers and benefactors.
- We return evil for evil, in which there is no sin, for it is necessary to pay a wicked man in his coin.
- One should not trust the sweet words of evil people because they do not forget their original nature. A tiger does not leave violence.
- Don't be kind to harmful people.
- An evil person thinks of everyone who follows the path of righteousness as his enemy; yet a gentleman continues on his righteous path.
- There is poison in the fang of the serpent, in the mouth of the fly and in the sting of a scorpion; but the wicked man is saturated with it.
- If you were to choose between an evil person and a snake to keep company with, opt for the snake. Because the snake will bite you only in self-defence but the evil person will put bite for any reason and at any time or always.
- There are only two ways of dealing with evil persons or thorns. Crush them under your boot or stay far away from them.
- The Neem tree (a bitter tree), even when irrigated with ghee, milk and sugar, does not change its nature,

i.e., does not shun its bitterness; much in the same manner, it is not possible to reform an evil person into a gentleman despite all sermons and affectionate treatment.

- A person who refrains from charity, who thinks that the study of the Vedas is a wasteful pastime, who thinks a visit to saints and ascetics is pointless, who has never visited religious places, who has amassed wealth immorally, who remains behind the facade of arrogance and vanity all the time, is degenerate, evil and selfish. He only lives for himself and is not concerned with others.
- An evil person cannot keep a secret; he spreads it all over in no time.
- An evil and cruel person's behaviour changes mysteriously according to circumstances. So, it is impossible for anyone to understand it.
- An evil person is like a dead weight on the earth. He is better dead than alive. He should better relinquish his life at the earliest, otherwise, he will only promote sin and wrong-doing.
- Eschew wicked company and associates with saintly persons. Acquire virtue day and night, and always meditate on that which is eternal forgetting that which is temporary.
- Like a wild pumpkin cannot turn sweet even after fully ripening, that is, it continues to be bitter, an

evil person, howsoever aged he may be, retains his cruel and sinful nature. Even at an elderly age, he continues to scheme. So, a man should be judged by his abilities rather than his age.

- It is the basic nature of an evil person to envy the progress of others. He tries to work for his own advancement, without caring if it hurts others. But when he fails, he resorts to criticizing in order to uplift himself and degrade others. This is how he tries to prove himself an able person.
- Like a snake, a honeybee and a scorpion possess poison, an evil person is also equipped with deadly poison the only difference is that the snake's poison is in its fangs, the honeybee's poison in its forehead and the scorpion's poison is in its tail; whereas the evil person's entire body is poisonous. Anyone, who comes into his contact, cannot escape from his evil effect.
- An evil and cruel person is satisfied with harming others. He feels elated in seeing others in crisis.
- An evil person can be identified by his extreme anger, utter poisonous speech and ever readiness to cause harm to friends and relations. Such a person keeps the company of evil people and works for contemptible men. Such a person bears extreme hardships of hell, even while living in this world.

- An elephant is controlled by an iron goad, a horse by a whip and a horned animal by a stick, much like these, to control an evil person, one needs to use a sword (punishment). An evil person possesses a very low mentality. He is always scheming to harm others. It is impossible to transform such people with love, affection and knowledge.

Wife

- A woman, who delivers happiness to her husband, can, in fact, be called a wife.
- A woman, who is pure, clever and wise; who is prudently devoted; who only loves her husband; who always speaks the truth and shuns lies, only that woman is worthy and fit for the home.
- For an aged person, a young wife is like poison.
- The wife is a true companion in old age and her absence makes a man completely helpless.
- One's wife, even if she is ugly or beautiful, evil or amiable, foolish or intelligent, should not be deserted. If he is satisfied with her, he will be free from mental tension forever.
- A good wife is one who serves her husband in the morning like a mother does, loves him in the day like a sister does and pleases him like a prostitute in the night.

Wisdom

- Patient, mature, wise gentlemen maintain their cool even in adverse circumstances and try to resolve their difficulties with determination.
- Methods and techniques of governance can be learnt from the texts but the wisdom of the aged and experienced provides accurate practical knowledge. When theory and practice come together. It is called wisdom.
- The wise man should restrain his senses like the crane and accomplish his purpose with due knowledge of his place, time and ability.
- Controlling all your senses like the Heron, and after carefully considering the factors of time and space as well the capacity of the Self, the wise accomplish their work successfully.
- The difficulties in work borne by men should be solved with wisdom.
- Wisdom is useful in a crisis.
- Flowers have fragrance, seeds have oil, wood burns, milk contains ghee and sugarcane is sweet, all these qualities are not visible. Similarly, in the case of men, the soul is present in the body but cannot be seen. However, it can be felt by wisdom. So, a man should enlighten it with wisdom.

Women

- A physically beautiful woman can give you pleasure for only one night. But a mentally beautiful woman will give you for a lifetime. It is a good idea to accept a person who is beautiful from the mind.
- A woman's strength lies in her beauty, youth and sweet talks. She may be delicate, yet it is through these that she has the power to make anyone bow before her.
- Whoever looks at women in a bad way will never be holy. He invites his own decline.
- It is imprudent to advise a fool, care for a woman with bad character and to be in the company of a lethargic and unhappy person.
- An adulteress is the enemy of her children.
- Needy and resourceless women can fall into bad company and lose their character and respect. So, they should refrain from travelling needlessly.
- Nobody is as radiant as a loyal woman.
- A shameless woman from a high-status family when falls in bad company, she ruins herself and her family.
- Closeness to a woman generates many flaws, whereas separation might cause her to go astray. To safeguard from this situation, a man should take a middle path.

He should remain neither too close nor too far from her.

- A loyal woman who is continuously dedicated to serving her husband, need not donate, fast, visit holy shrines or take a dip in holy rivers. In fact, being devoted to serving her husband by itself purifies her.

Work

- By just wishing, no work will be completed. No prey will enter a lion's mouth on its own. So, we have to work hard to fulfil our desires.
- Do tomorrow's work today.
- The power of hard work is limitless; its strength can even make possible the impossible. So, a man should not shy away from hard work; rather he should make all possible efforts and by untiring hard work, make his life happy.
- A person who is aware of future troubles, and fights against them with his intelligence, will be always happy. And a person who remains inactive (without working) waiting for good days to come, will destroy his own life.
- No work is too difficult or impossible for people who are powerful, capable and courageous.

- One must publicize only that work which is complete and successful.
- He who discerns the right time of doing work, gets sure success.
- Doing work flawlessly is a rare happening.
- Do not be very upright in your dealings, for you would see by going to the forest, that straight trees are cut down while crooked ones are left standing.
- One must complete one's job in due time because any delay may not let one complete it at all.
- Not using the available means properly interferes with completing the work.
- Whether it be big or small, we must do every work with our full capacity and power. We must learn this quality from the lion. A lion never does anything halfheartedly, whether it is attacking a rabbit or an elephant, with equal ferocity.
- Start any work after assessing totally your capability for doing it.
- People, who stray from their planned and feasible tasks and jump to unplanned and unachievable tasks, never succeed. They should, therefore, attempt only those tasks, which they are confident of achieving.

- The job must be assigned on the basis of the expertise of its plausible performers.
- A work is completed if one is determined to do it. Then it becomes one's sole aim.
- A person should feel satisfied with whatever he earns through hard work.

❑

Yajna

- While performing the yajna grains should be donated, the hymns should be recited according to the laid-down procedure and priests should be given a proper honorarium. If this does not happen, the yajna can cause ruin. So, the yajna should only be performed when the capability to perform it as per the correct procedures exists.

❑

References

1. www.speakingtree.in/
2. www.chanakya-quotes.blogspot.in/
3. www.viralknot.com/
4. www.scoopwhoop.com/
5. www.achhikhabar.com/
6. www.chanakya.brainhungry.com/
7. www.patheos.com/
8. www.nationalviews.com/
9. www.brainyquote.com/
10. www.chanakya.brainhungry.com/
11. www.hindutva.info/
12. www.invajy.com/
13. www.imvoyager.com/
14. www.quoteshindi.net/

❑❑❑